WESTERN NEW YORK
····· *and the* ·····
GILDED AGE

WESTERN NEW YORK
····and the····
GILDED AGE

JULIANNA FIDDLER-WOITE
···MARY BETH PAULIN SCUMACI···
PETER C. SCUMACI

THE
History
PRESS

Published by The History Press
Charleston, SC 29403
www.historypress.net

Select cover images provided by the Traveling Picture Show
All other images are from the authors' collections unless otherwise noted.

First published 2010

Manufactured in the United States

ISBN 978.1.59629.982.5

Library of Congress Cataloging-in-Publication Data

Fiddler-Woite, Julianna.
Western New York and the Gilded Age / Julianna Fiddler-Woite, Mary Beth Paulin
Scumaci and Peter C. Scumaci.
p. cm.
Includes bibliographical references.
ISBN 978-1-59629-982-5
1. New York (State), Western--History--19th century--Pictorial works. 2. New York
(State), Western--Pictorial works. 3. Postcards--New York (State), Western. 4. New
York (State)--History--1865---Pictorial works. I. Scumaci, Mary Beth Paulin. II.
Scumaci, Peter C. III. Title.
F126.9.F53 2010
974.7--dc22
2010017224

Notice: The information in this book is true and complete to the best of our
knowledge. It is offered without guarantee on the part of the authors or The History
Press. The authors and The History Press disclaim all liability in connection with the
use of this book.

For my mom, Lois Landel Fiddler, who is quietly responsible for all the things I accomplish.
For Rob, Mitchell, Laceyanne, Wendy and Victoria, who always pretend to be interested.
And as always, in memory of my dad, Robert C. Fiddler, who first inspired my love for all things historical.

—Julianna Fiddler-Woite

———

For Kenneth and Virginia Paulin, thank you for your love, dedication and a great education.
For Peter, Allie and Ryan, you light up my world and make me smile every day.
In loving memory of Ben and Kathryn Paulin and Joe and Loretto Rundle, thank you for the memories. Your spirit lives on.

—Mary Beth Paulin Scumaci

———

To my wonderful wife, Mary Beth, and beautiful children, Allison and Ryan, for their unending support and love.
To my big brother, Robert, for his knowledge, artistry and friendship.
To my mother and father, Joan and Bob Scumaci, for turning a basement closet into a darkroom and starting it all.

—Peter C. Scumaci

CONTENTS

Acknowledgements

Amherst Central Alumni Foundation (ACAF)
David Carson
Nannette Rundle Carroll
Tracey DiNicolantonio
Caroline Duax
Lois Fiddler
Frank Godson
Kevin P. Maria
North Tonawanda History Museum (NTHM)
Kenneth and Virginia Paulin
Paula Rankin
Kim Retallack
Isabel Robitaille
Bob Scumaci
Virginia Sharp
Dorothy and Bill Shaver
St. Paul's Lutheran Church, Williamsville
Traveling Picture Show (TPS, www.travelingpictureshow.com)

Introduction

The Gilded Age

The Gilded Age in Western New York (WNY) was a time of discovery, prosperity, growth and fellowship. Born from the success of the Erie Canal, the WNY community flourished throughout the 1800s and early 1900s. By the turn of the century, Buffalo had become the eighth largest city in America and housed several of the country's wealthiest citizens. In 1901, Buffalo's streets were lined with immaculate landscaping and the world's first electrical streetlights, earning it the titles "City of Trees" and "City of Light." In the suburbs, neighborhoods grew, farmers prospered and small businesses increased. As a region, WNY sent two men to the White House and witnessed the assassination of one president and the inauguration of another. All over WNY, life was fruitful, and the communities enjoyed the spoils.

At the heart of it all, however, were the people themselves. A century and a half later, Buffalo is known as the "City of Good Neighbors," and the region is still close-knit and proud. What is chronicled in this book is timeless. Sewn together from family photographs and vintage postcards, this book cleverly details everyday life in WNY. This work offers a glimpse into where people worked, who they knew and how they played. While some of their circumstances are unique, many of their adventures mimic those of the present day. This is the beauty of WNY. Faces may change, buildings may crumble and empires may fall, but for every lost landmark, a treasure remains. So take a few minutes to walk in the footprints left by WNY's grand forefathers. You just might discover that we are not so different after all.

The Buffalo Lighthouse was built in 1833 and still serves as a poignant symbol of WNY's history and prosperity. *Photography by Peter Scumaci.*

Chapter 1

Big Business

Although settlements existed in Western New York (WNY) previously, the true birth of the region can be traced to 1823, when digging began for the Buffalo portion of the Erie Canal. Over the next twenty years, the population of WNY increased by 145 percent, and the business landscape changed dramatically. Now, scattered among WNY's ordinary residents were some of the most powerful men in the nation. Their stories were captivating and their impact eternal.

Prominent Businessmen

William G. Fargo (1818–1881)

The Buffalo waterfront was the focal point of many successful businesses in the 1800s. In 1844, William G. Fargo began a legendary express business with partner Henry Wells. By 1851, Wells Fargo & Co. had a monopoly on the express industry, expanded to railroad shipping and proudly delivered between San Francisco and New York. Wells Fargo soon became a staple of American culture and will forever be celebrated by the song "The Wells Fargo Wagon" from Meredith Wilson's *The Music Man*.

As a result of his wealth and success, Fargo was elected mayor of Buffalo in 1861. In 1870, he completed construction of his new home, which was one of the most elaborate and costly mansions in the state. The Fargo Mansion covered two city blocks, from Pennsylvania Avenue and West Avenue to Jersey Street and Fargo Avenue. The home, which contained a five-story tower, was the first in the city to have an elevator. The dwelling was said to have golden doorknobs and contain wood from all states in the Union.

John Blocher (1825–1911)

John Blocher was a Civil War soldier who served in New York's 78th Regiment. Upon returning to WNY, Blocher began manufacturing shoes and boots, dabbling in real estate and opening breweries. By the 1870s, he had become one of Buffalo's wealthiest citizens. Professionally, however, Blocher is most often associated with his vision of "a home where aging men and women may enjoy their senior years." The Blocher Homes opened in Williamsville in 1906. This facility remained a staple of the village landscape for generations and is presently operated by Beechwood.

Despite their business success, the Blochers may best be remembered for the Blocher Mausoleum in Forest Lawn Cemetery and the fascinating story behind its creation. The legendary tale revolves around Nelson Blocher and the family's Irish maid, Katherine, with whom Nelson was in love. Disapproving of Nelson's feelings, however, his parents sent him overseas in 1881, and the maid was dismissed. Upon his return in 1882, Nelson was shocked to discover that his love was gone and all that remained behind was her Bible. Heartbroken, Nelson canvassed the globe throughout 1883 but never found her. Exhausted and sick with fever, Nelson eventually took to his bed. He died on January 24, 1884, with Katherine's Bible clutched to his chest.

Riddled with guilt, the Blochers commissioned the infamous mausoleum as a tribute to their only son. Constructed of Italian marble, the monument displays Nelson on his deathbed, flanked by his parents, John and Elizabeth. Nelson clings to a Bible, and an angel hovers overhead. The angel, it was said, was likened after the Blochers' maid, Katherine. Clearly, the symbolism is as rich as the architecture.

Darwin D. Martin (1865–1935) and Frank Lloyd Wright (1867–1959)

Darwin D. Martin was born in Bouckville, New York, and left home at age thirteen to work as a soap slinger for the Larkin Soap Company. Impressing the company leaders with his strong work ethic, Martin was brought to Buffalo, where he became an executive in the Larkin administration. By 1902, Martin had become a millionaire and forged a working relationship and friendship with aspiring architect Frank Lloyd Wright. He commissioned Wright to begin work on his personal estate in 1902 and the new Larkin Administrative Building in 1904.

The friendship of Darwin D. Martin and Frank Lloyd Wright is forever evident at 125 Jewett Parkway in the city of Buffalo. This location, which is within the Parkside East Historic District, was designed by renowned landscape architect Fredrick Law Olmsted. Martin purchased the property in 1902, and Wright began construction in 1903. The resulting Darwin D. Martin Complex was added to the National Registry of Historic Places in 1975 and became a National Historic Landmark in 1986.

Wright remained Martin's friend throughout his lifetime and stood by him when the stock market crash eliminated his fortune. The men attempted various business partnerships, but none came to fruition. Following Martin's death, the estate was abandoned by his destitute widow and remained vacant for two decades.

E.G. Spaulding (1809–1897)

One of the wealthiest figures of early WNY was banker and politician E.G. Spaulding. In 1847, E.G. Spaulding was voted mayor of Buffalo and eventually served in Congress as a member of the Whig Party. Throughout his political career, Spaulding was a staunch supporter of Abraham Lincoln and proudly hosted a congratulatory dinner at the National Hotel in Washington, D.C., following his election.

Outside of politics, E.G. Spaulding was prominent in the banking business, operating Spaulding Bank on the second floor of the Spaulding Exchange, one of the finest buildings of its time. Located at 162 Main Street, the Spaulding Exchange would later be torn down to make room for the Memorial Auditorium.

Regardless of the travels of his political career, the WNY area remained Spaulding's home, and he owned elaborate mansions in both Buffalo and Grand Island. On the homefront, Spaulding married three times and was widowed by each. Next to presidents Grover Cleveland and Millard Fillmore, Spaulding was Buffalo's most illustrious citizen of his era. At the time of his death, his estate was worth over $4 million, making him Buffalo's wealthiest citizen.

THE AUTOMOBILE INDUSTRY

E.G. Spaulding's granddaughter, Edith, joined another of Buffalo's prominent families when she wed William Allen Gardner. William's grandfather, Noah Gardner, was one of the incorporators of the Buffalo Savings Bank and had amassed quite a fortune. According to the 1912 *Genealogical and Family History of Western New York*, William's father, William Hamilton Gardner, was prominent in the automobile industry and served as director of the Pierce Arrow Motor Car Company.

In the early part of the twentieth century, the Pierce Arrow Motor Car Company produced some of the most luxurious automobiles on the market. The company, however, began as a bicycle manufacturer and did not venture into autos until the Pan-American Exposition of 1901. At that time, George N. Pierce & Company built two cars and submitted them for exhibition at the exposition's opening. The Pierce Motorette was a two-and-three-quarters-horsepower automobile with a maximum speed of fifteen miles per hour. According to the local paper, "Crowds parted, eyes popped and jaws dropped as the contraption clattered past."

Following his success, Pierce continued to operate from the same bicycle plant on Hanover Street for several years. By 1907, the auto production had moved to a plant on Elmwood Avenue at Great Arrow. Enjoying unparalleled success throughout the Roaring Twenties, Pierce Arrow ultimately closed its doors in 1938, when the Great Depression finally took its toll on the luxury automaker.

Thus, by the early twentieth century, the age of the automobile had officially begun. Originally only a folly for the wealthy, "gas buggies" gradually became more common on the streets of WNY. This necessitated the opening of new types of businesses to cater to the needs of the automobile and its driver. Gas stations and mechanics' shops began to replace blacksmiths and wagon works. A new era in WNY—symbolized by the electric lights that were installed on Main Street in 1901—had truly begun, and many people were able to profit from it.

SMALL BUSINESSES

The success of the Erie Canal bolstered business in the city of Buffalo, as well as in the individual business districts in emerging communities. The retail and hospitality industries were booming, and companies hired large numbers of workers of both sexes. Grand hotels were filled to capacity during the Pan-American Exposition, and their food and retail counterparts profited greatly. It was a golden era, and the people of WNY enjoyed the prosperity and company of their fellow workers.

Breweries were a common business in the suburbs as well as in the city. In 1845, John Blocher and George Urban opened a brewery on Main Street near Grove in Williamsville. This brewery changed hands several times and was known as the Williamsville Co-op Brewing Association in 1884, the Amherst Brewery Lager Beer in 1895 and the Erie County Brewing Company in 1897.

Rapidly changing technology allowed for new business opportunities in the suburbs. Along with automobiles, the advent of the telephone was big business at the turn of the century. For instance, when the first telephone lines were installed from Buffalo to Williamsville in 1879, only four homes had units. By 1905, however, forty homes had requested sets, and Frontier Telephone Co. was granted franchising rights. Concurrently, private phone sales and repairmen began to surface in the suburbs, and a whole new line of business products emerged.

CONSTRUCTION

The growth of the WNY population brought incredible opportunities for those in the construction business. Work was needed for commercial, as well as residential, projects, as communities built homes, churches, schools and businesses to accommodate the flood of new residents. Without the luxury of telephones, arrangements for work had to be made through postcards and letters:

March 19, 1910–Clarence
To: Landel Bros–Williamsville
Dear Sir—
I haven't hired out yet so I will come out to see you the first part of next week to see whether we can make bargain.
From Henry Ronicker

Farming

Farming remained the principal means of support for many suburban communities throughout the 1800s and early 1900s. Orchards, crops and livestock were stable means of income, as was the practice of selling firewood to the City of Buffalo. The suburbs would sell their crops within their communities as well as through larger farmers' markets in the city. Schools would even adjust their schedules to allow children to help at home with the harvest.

Above: The home of William G. Fargo, co-founder of Wells Fargo & Co. and the American Express Company.

Right: A unique piece of the Fargo Mansion's banister is housed at the Buffalo & Erie County Historical Society.

The original Blocher Homes building as it appeared on Evans Street in the early 1900s.

Blocher lived at 168 Delaware Avenue in a mansion purchased in 1878. Here he resided with his wife, Katherine, and son, Nelson.

The Blocher Mausoleum in Forest Lawn Cemetery. The granite exterior, as well as the marble figures on the interior, was designed by John Blocher, who had no formal architectural training. *Photography by Peter Scumaci.*

While the figures depict the deathbed scene of Nelson Blocher, the actual remains of the Blocher family are entombed in a crypt beneath the floor. The vault is accessed by sliding Nelson and the couch sideways. *Photography by Peter Scumaci.*

Frank Lloyd Wright's Prairie-style Darwin D. Martin Complex encompasses 29,080 square feet and includes the Martin House, the Barton House, the Carriage House, the Gardner's Cottage, the Conservatory and the Pergola. *Photography by Peter Scumaci.*

Opposite, top: The Spaulding Mansion was located at the southeast corner of Main and Goodell Streets. Pictured is the sitting room. This mansion would be torn down after his death and the Sideway Building erected in its place.

Opposite, bottom: Spaulding's daughter, Charlotte, and her husband, Franklin Sideway, inherited the Spauldings' Grand Island property and mansion. This property was later taken over by the state to form Beaver Island State Park. *Courtesy of David Carson.*

E.G. Spaulding is buried in the family lot in Forest Lawn Cemetery, at the site of the cenotaph he dedicated in honor of the nine Spaulding veterans of the Battle of Bunker Hill. *Photography by Peter Scumaci.*

William Hamilton Gardner (1842–1915). *Courtesy of David Carson.*

The Pierce Arrow Motor Car Company.

The Black Rock Garage, located in Buffalo's historic Black Rock section, also housed Black Rock Taxi and dealt United States Tires.

This photograph, labeled "garage help," indicates that even the employees at the Black Rock Garage dressed in proper fashion.

International Harvester manufactured agricultural machinery and vehicles. Mechanic John B. Schoelles of Williamsville (right) surveys a single-cylinder pump, known as the "one lunger," in 1911.

In many communities, small factory jobs became easy to come by, as evidenced by these machine shop workers from the early 1900s.

The Hamill Company, located on Delaware and Eagle Streets, employed a large number of people in their plumbers' supply business.

The Hamill employees enjoy a day off together at the Hamill family's home at Crystal Beach.

Hotel waitresses Eva, Laura and Beatrice enjoy their hotel's proximity to Lake Erie.

Webster Street in North Tonawanda (1884) housed many of the area's businesses. *Courtesy of NTHM.*

CHALMER'S

(FORMERLY WITH
J. & G. COX, SCOTLAND)

GELATINE.

SUPERIOR TO AND MUCH CHEAPER THAN THE IMPORTED.

Ask your grocer for our 2-oz. packet, and take no other.

JAMES CHALMERS' SON,
WILLIAMSVILLE, N. Y.

Chalmer's Gelatine was formed in 1872 by James and Peter Chalmers. Owners of the first manufacturing industry to operate out of Amherst, the brothers took advantage of a natural spring and built their business on Evans Street in Williamsville. *Courtesy of Kevin Maria.*

Big Business

Located on Franklin Street, this warehouse served as storage for Chalmer's Gelatine. At the time, food gelatin was used for various culinary products, including jellied salads, meats, ice cream, marshmallows and candy.

This collection of treasures provided by Kevin Maria showcases bottle openers from the Iroquois Brewing Company, as well as bottles from the Pan-American Exposition and breweries in Lancaster, Amherst, Williamsville, Buffalo and Tonawanda. *Photography by Peter Scumaci.*

A member of the Landel family proudly showcases the "Landel Bros. Williamsville and Buffalo Express Phones" vehicle.

Charles Landel and company work on the construction of a house for Edward Cotton of Gowanda.

Opposite, top: This image of the Landel construction crew shows the outfit's owner, Charles Landel, at the far right.

Opposite, bottom: By the end of the Roaring Twenties, opportunities in the construction business had become increasingly sparse. This image of the construction of Amherst High School in 1929 shows a sign hung on the work shack reading, "No help wanted." *Courtesy of ACAF.*

This image dated July 28, 1930, shows crews putting the finishing touches on Amherst High School. *Courtesy of ACAF.*

The Landel Farm, owned by Fred and Julianna Knoche Landel, was located on Main Street in Clarence.

Opposite, top: The Landels raised dairy cows, as well as other livestock, and grew corn and potatoes.

Opposite, middle: Arthur Landel, son of Fred and Julianna, operated his own dairy from his house at 5864 Main Street and would deliver the dairy products via his Williamsville Dairy milk wagon.

Opposite, bottom: The Washington Street Market was located parallel to Ellicott and perpendicular to Chippewa Street. It was one of the largest markets of the time.

Chapter 2

POLITICS AND PATRIOTISM

Through two wars and five presidents, Buffalo has found itself at the crossroads of history. Many famous figures, such as Presidents Abraham Lincoln, Grover Cleveland, William McKinley, Theodore Roosevelt and Millard Fillmore, have left their political marks on Buffalo and surrounding areas during the Gilded Age—marks that are still visible today.

PAN-AMERICAN EXPOSITION, MAY 1–NOVEMBER 1901

The Pan-American Exposition of 1901 was a joyous celebration of architectural design, technology, fashion and flare. The grounds were a disposable community built for education, entertainment and excitement. All buildings were constructed out of plaster except for the New York State Building, which is known today as the Erie County Historical Society. For the festivities, women dressed in long coats and dresses while men sported jackets, ties and bowlers. A spectacular display of lights lit up the evening sky. In the end, over eight million people traveled to visit the grand event.

A colossal statue of the Chariot Race greeted visitors at the entrance to the expo. The grounds were decorated with trees, shrubs and flowers to beautify the landscape. There were hundreds of stunning sculptures, extravagant buildings of differing colors and architectural designs and amazing water displays. Most impressive was the seventy-foot waterfall that flowed from the base of the Electric Tower. The U.S. Government Ordnance Exhibit displayed a variety of military cannons. There was even a space exhibit that simulated traveling to the moon and back, complete with children dressed as space creatures. Camel rides added to the exotic flare of the day.

ASSASSINATION ATTEMPT OF PRESIDENT WILLIAM MCKINLEY

September 6, 1901, was a somber day at the fair and ultimately marked the downfall of the Pan-American Exposition. While enjoying the ambiance of the elegant Temple of Music, President William McKinley was shot by a politically disgruntled Leon Czolgosz. Immediately, the president was rushed to the Pan-American hospital by an electric ambulance. He underwent surgery to retrieve the bullets and was later taken to the Milburn home to recover. Unfortunately, Dr. Roswell Park, Buffalo's finest physician, was out of town and could not tend to the president. Ultimately, complications from the surgery led to President McKinley's death eight days later.

Across the country, people were outraged by the assassination of their president, and violent mob attacks took place against Czolgosz to avenge his heinous crime. He was tried, found guilty and then transported to a prison in Auburn for electrocution. The gun that Czolgosz used is housed at the Erie County Historical Society.

Upon the death of President McKinley, Theodore Roosevelt was quickly and secretly sworn into office at the Ansley Wilcox home. Due to an altercation with a photographer, the only camera on site was broken. Hence, there were no photographs taken to document this historical occasion.

OTHER WESTERN NEW YORK PRESIDENTIAL CONNECTIONS

A precocious letter from a child connects Abraham Lincoln to WNY. In 1860, eleven-year-old Grace Bedell wrote to Lincoln telling him that his chances of being elected to the presidency would increase if he grew whiskers to hide his thin face. Lincoln responded to Grace by letter as well as in person. On the way to his presidential inauguration, he stopped at the train station in Westfield sporting a beard. When Lincoln stepped off the train, he met and thanked Bedell for her suggestion. A statue commemorating the famous meeting stands in Lincoln-Bedell Park in the village of Westfield in Chautauqua County.

Tributes to three other presidents can also be found around the streets of WNY. Buffalo native Millard Fillmore, our country's thirteenth president, is prominently remembered through a variety of buildings that memorialize his name and spirit. The buildings include Millard Fillmore Gates Hospital, Millard Fillmore Suburban Hospital, the Buffalo Club, the Stattler Building and a monument that stands in his honor in the Forest Lawn Cemetery. Theodore Roosevelt Plaza is located at Main and Heuron Streets in Buffalo and honors the twenty-sixth president of the United States. The plaza includes the Buffalo Savings Bank, the Hiker Statue, the Niagara Tower and the Genesee Building. Additionally, statues of both Buffalo presidents, Millard Fillmore and Grover Cleveland, adorn Buffalo's city hall.

FORTS, ARMORIES AND RUINS

Buffalo and the surrounding area did a booming business due to the local waterways. It was a natural location for military training grounds, forts and hospitals. Located in Lewiston, Fort Niagara was built in 1679 by the French and used as a military foothold in the area. The French Castle, the center building of the fort, was built in 1726. Americans took control of the fort in 1796 after defeating the British during the Revolutionary War. The fort and surrounding areas became the training grounds for military troops for the Spanish-American War (1898), the Philippine Insurrection (1899–1901) and World War I (1914–17).

The influence of patriotism and loyalty to the United States was demonstrated repeatedly throughout the years. Arsenals, forts and armories were necessary for training and storage of military equipment. Judge Joseph Masten, namesake of the Masten Street Armory, has a fascinating history. Cemetery Street of Buffalo was renamed Masten Street in 1897 in his honor, and he served as the first democratic mayor of Buffalo from 1843 to 1847. He served as a Superior Court judge from 1856 to 1871. Masten eventually purchased a military fort at Delaware and North Streets and turned it into a residence that is known as the Ansley Wilcox Mansion, the inaugural site of President Theodore Roosevelt. The Masten Street Armory was built in 1907 and burned down in 1931. The adjutant general reported that "this was one of the largest and finest armories in the country, and its loss was a heavy blow." The Connecticut Street Armory was built in 1898 and was primarily used for training purposes. The cost of the armory was $400,000.

A TRIBUTE TO WESTERN NEW YORK SOLDIERS

The number of memorials and monuments in WNY is representative of the pride and patriotism of the people. Citizens appreciated that the life of a soldier was dangerous work that took men away from their families for extended periods of time. During such times, communication was important in keeping families connected. Without cellphones and e-mail, postcards and letters enabled soldiers and loved ones to keep in touch with one another. They described their enemies and gave descriptions of fighting the war, disease and loneliness, all while trying to cheer and support their loved ones from afar.

The following excerpts take us into the minds and thoughts of three World War I soldiers: Cyrus Schoelles and cousins Arthur and Herman Landel.

June 7, 1918—Morrison, Virginia
Dear Sis, Bro and Babe—
Has Art gone to war or haven't they been called yet? I suppose the truck business is rising now. Charlie will only have to work about 24 hours a day. Well that's not so bad. In the Army "over there" they work about 48.
Well we got the subs over here now and they're not far away either. We heard the horn of a big boat last night at midnight but haven't heard

whether a sub got it or not. The sub got one close by on Wed. The survivors are at Newport News.
We'll close with love to all.
Answer soon—Cy
Enclosed find $5.00. Bank it.

Aug 28, 1918—Florence S.C.
Dear Bro.—
Arrived here about 7 this morning. Are laying over for breakfast. Scenery was fine till Baltimore but fear the country from Washington south. Supper at Richmond Va last night. Will reach Georgia tonight. Art

August 7, 1919—San Diego
I mailed you a package—keep it for me. Enjoying liberty here today after 10 days at sea. Nice climate and place, fruit galore. People gave us a great welcome—right through the earthquake last Sunday. Fun and excitement after nothing happening for a while and no subs to look after. Herman

August 16, 1919—Los Angeles
Having a great time here. People gave us a great welcome and I fear are spoiling the sailors. Everyone has a car out here. Never saw so many girls before either. Have to watch my step, would lose my head sure if I wasn't an old timer at the girl questions. Ha! Herman

Scarlet Fever Attacks the Troops
Camp Hancock—November 22, 1918
Dear Brother
It has been some time since I wrote to you, but I suppose you heard that they sent me to the base hospital. I can truthfully say that I have never found a place in all my life where news was so scarce as it has been here. What a place to be stationed in for three weeks. This is how long they say we are quarantined for. Well I have nearly two weeks in and I can stand another week if they will let me out at that time. I was a little sick when they sent me over here, but didn't want to write it home or mother would have worried.

I will tell you that Scarlet Fever struck our company hard. When our men began to get sick they sent 20 men to the hospital in 2 days. Of course I don't want you to tell mother this, but shortly after the fellows came over I began to lose appetite but I stuck it out for 4 days and didn't eat a thing.

On the 5th day, the captain came over and looked at my throat, turned around and walked out of the tent. I heard him say "A sure case of Scarlet Fever, one of the worst we have. Send him over to the Base Hospital." I didn't feel very sick, but my temperature was up to 103 degrees. I came over here and went to bed. I got up the second day but couldn't eat anything for a week. I feel fine now but heard pretty sad new this A.M. Four of our men died—all good friends of mine—one fellow especially, John Kelley from New York City. They say he died Monday and they shipped the body Tuesday. I will tell you this is tough at the least when we are so near the end. You hadn't better tell mother about the deaths of these fellows. I don't think there is any more danger, but she would only worry about it.

I suppose my little niece is getting to be the limit by now. I sure would like to see her. I often miss her and Eunice for I used to fool with them so much and now I haven't seen a kid in 3 months!
Best wishes to all.
Brother Art

A Soldier's Christmas Away from Home
Camp Hancock—Christmas 1918
Dear Mother,
I have about an hour so I will write a few lines on our greatest day of the year. I hope that all of you have recovered from your attack of the flu and that you could all be together to see the two little ones enjoying themselves. When I think of them in connection with Christmas, I always think of how I used to stand on the church benches and watch the children on Christmas Eve. I think that last night was the first Christmas Eve that I didn't attend church since I can remember. Instead I walked post on guard last night and all day so it made it a very long Christmas.

They celebrate Christmas Eve much different here from what we do up home. I walked from 12 until 2 this A.M. and they celebrated in town much as we do New Year's Eve.

I met the Lutheran Camp Pastor while at the Base Hospital and he invited me to services and out to dinner today, but of course I couldn't go. We had a fine dinner here in the company which made the day very pleasant. Of course there were very few presents on account of the boys not knowing when they will be going home and a lot of them thought that they would be going before this. The "O.S. Training" are going to leave in the morning and I expect we will be leaving soon after that if they don't send us to work at some arsenal.

I am quite anxious to hear if Chas is able and around. Now if he isn't I will try and get an immediate discharge. It seems foolish that I should be lying around here when I could just as well be helping out at home. If I want an immediate discharge I would have to have a doctor's certificate and a notary public's certificate stating that brother was physically unfit to handle business and I was needed at once.

I have received my OD clothing and will get a new overcoat tomorrow for the one they burnt by putting it through the sterilizer. My blouse and trousers don't match very well but I got new stuff and most of the boys got patched clothing. I had to have my trousers cut over at an expense of $1.25, but they fit fine now.

With Best Wishes to All—

Son Art

Our Friends and Relatives Across the Border Help During the War

Drawn from the memoir of Loretto Haffey Rundle is her recollection of being eleven years old and living in Welland, Canada, at the time of World War I. The memory illustrates the positive relationship between the United States and Canada during a difficult political time.

November 11, 1918

I was 11 years old when we moved to Batavia, New York. World War I started in 1914. It started in Germany and Great Britain. The fighting was in Europe. All countries became involved. Eventually the US entered the World War in 1917. Businesses that could be converted to make war supplies were common. Dad's brother, Uncle Joe was a manager of the munitions plant in Batavia, New York. My father, Jim Haffey, joined him as superintendent of the plant. He commuted from Welland, Ontario, Canada where we lived, to Batavia every week. He would come home on weekends.

My mother and father decided to move to Batavia. They rented out 64 Smith Street, leased it for a year. They moved some things like all the fruit and vegetables which mother had preserved in the fall. Our clothes and personal effects were moved by a mover. My mother had taken care of the immigration and all the details regarding customs, etc.

On the eleventh month, at the eleventh hour, November 11, 1918, a peace treaty was signed which ended World War I. It was called an

"Armistice" and for several years that date, November 11th, was remembered as "Armistice Day." The church bells rang out, the factory whistles blew and everyone was excited…the war was over!

Thus, politics and patriotism have threaded communities together over the years. From presidents and soldiers to families and communities, they all have a story to share, stories that have shaped and influenced our history as we know it today.

A postcard of an original ticket that provided entrance to the Pan-American Exposition of 1901. The small portion of the ticket was kept by the gate attendant while the large portion served as a souvenir. *Courtesy of TPS.*

The seating and water outside of the Machinery and Transportation Building at the Pan-American Exposition provide a peaceful setting. *Courtesy of TPS.*

An aerial view of the Pan-American Exposition Stadium from the Electric Tower. *Courtesy of TPS.*

Temple of Music,
Pan American
Exposition,
where President McKinley
was shot Sept. 6, 1901.

A postcard marks the day President McKinley was shot in the Temple of Music at the Pan-American Exposition. *Courtesy of TPS.*

President McKinley died a tragic death at the Milburn home on September 14, 1901. *Courtesy of TPS.*

Politics and Patriotism

A postcard image of the inauguration of Theodore Roosevelt on September 14, 1901. *Courtesy of TPS.*

Located on Delaware Avenue in Buffalo, the Ansley Wilcox home now serves as a historical museum honoring the memory of President William McKinley and the inauguration of President Theodore Roosevelt. *Photography by Peter Scumaci.*

A tribute to a young Abraham Lincoln presides over Delaware Park in the 1920s.

This statue of "Lincoln the Emancipator" was dedicated in 1902 and presently sits on the portico steps of the Erie County Historical Society. *Photography by Peter Scumaci.*

Statues honor the meeting of President Lincoln and the "Little Girl," Grace Bedell, who wrote to him requesting that he grow whiskers to raise his popularity and chances for winning the presidential election. *Photography by Peter Scumaci.*

The New York State Building, now the Buffalo and Erie County Historical Society, has a rich presidential history. President McKinley dined in this building the day before he was shot, and President Millard Fillmore was the founder and first president of the historical society. *Courtesy of TPS.*

The Millard Fillmore Monument located in Forest Lawn Cemetery honoring the life of our thirteenth president. *Photography by Peter Scumaci.*

The Buffalo Club, located on Delaware Avenue, was founded in 1867 by Millard Fillmore, who served as its first president. United States president Grover Cleveland was a member from 1881 to 1906. In 1901, after the assassination attempt on President McKinley, it served as the headquarters for Vice President Theodore Roosevelt and the rest of McKinley's cabinet. *Photography by Peter Scumaci.*

Buffalo Savings Bank and its gold dome cost $300,000 to build. The Hiker Statue across the street is dedicated to the American soldiers who served in the Spanish-American War, the Philippine Insurrection and the Boxer Rebellion. Theodore Roosevelt was finally awarded the Medal of Honor in 2001, more than one hundred years after the Spanish-American War. *Photography by Peter Scumaci.*

The architecture of the Niagara Tower was inspired by the Electric Tower of the Pan-American Exposition of 1901. The tower was designed by Esenwein & Johnson and built in 1912. *Photography by Peter Scumaci.*

Opposite, top: A 1920s photo of Fort Niagara located in Lewiston.

Opposite, middle: Fort Niagara restored to its original façade.

Opposite, bottom: Tourists relax while visiting the historical site.

The 65th Arsenal on Broadway played an important role in organizing troops for the

After World War I, patriotism and American pride were strong. Military forts, armories and cannons became popular tourist attractions.

Several retired cannons were positioned around WNY, including this one in Delaware Park.

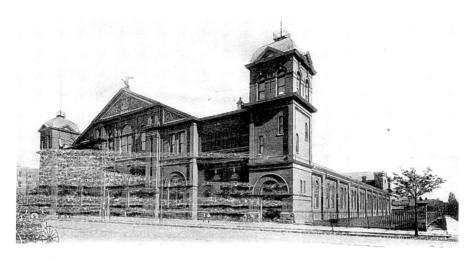

The 65th Arsenal on Broadway played an important role in organizing troops for the Spanish-American War of 1898. *Courtesy of TPS.*

The ruins of Fort Porter on Porter Road in Buffalo served as a guard and customhouse. They were located near where the Peace Bridge stands today. *Courtesy of TPS.*

The U.S. Marine Hospital of Buffalo was used for treating soldiers who were wounded or fell ill during World War I.

A postcard of the 65th Regiment Armory, or Masten Street Armory. *Courtesy of TPS.*

A photo of the Masten Street Armory as it stands today after being rebuilt in 1933. *Photography by Peter Scumaci.*

A postcard illustration of the 74th Regiment Armory, circa 1898.

Above: A current photo of the 74th Regiment Armory, or Connecticut Street Armory, as it stands today. *Photography by Peter Scumaci.*

Left: A statue of a World War I doughboy stands in recognition and honor of all soldiers who fought to protect the United States of America during World War I. The statue is located in front of the Connecticut Street Armory in Buffalo. *Photography by Peter Scumaci.*

A World War I soldier poses in uniform.

A soldier poses under the stone arch at the Gate House on Main Street, Snyder. *Courtesy of Caroline Duax.*

A portrait of World War I soldier Arthur Landel. The Landel family lived on a farm in Tonawanda on the Erie Canal before moving to Clarence.

Chapter 3

CREATING COMMUNITIES

B eyond business and politics lies the heart of WNY—the people. Woven together from places near and far, the WNY community was a tapestry of individuality. Together, people learned a common language, endured common enemies and formed common bonds. They worked together, played together, learned together and worshiped together. For them, WNY became a true home, and for many families, it has remained so for generations.

FAMILY, FRIENDS AND FASHION

No matter what the true geographical acreage, WNY was a small town. Family connections stretched wide and far, and friendships endured no matter what the distance. Events such as weddings and births were community affairs, and no guest list was ever necessary. Penny postcards made communication affordable, and the masses employed them in much the same way people today would send a quick text or e-mail.

July 27, 1910—Lockport
Charlie—I have three girls and can't string any of them. What do you think of it? J.S.

Nov 9, 1910—Clarence
Rather sorry election day. I suppose you walked up and pulled down the
lever. I didn't—still have to. I was out your way Sunday but there was no
light hanging out. You must have been sleeping. We came to Transit for a
young lady. Went to Harris Hill Church (with a gray flannel shirt on). I'll
tell you about it—she was a dandy. I have great heart trouble right now.

Depending on where you lived, the fashion of the day could differ greatly. In the country and suburbs, attire was closely associated with daily chores and workload. For many children, shoes were a nuisance and were reserved for Sunday services. Among the upper classes, fashion was a priority and its rules obeyed. For men, flannel was reserved for casual wear and tweed for sport. Ascot-style ties were to be worn during the day and bow ties at night. Hats were necessary whenever outdoors.

Women's hats, an essential part of any outfit, told the story of the changing times. As the wide-brim hats of the Victorian era gave way to the less pretentious bonnets of the Roaring Twenties, the world of fashion witnessed its greatest coup yet: the birth of the flapper. In a 1924 *Buffalo Sunday Times* interview, ninety-three-year-old Jacob Snyder gave his opinion of this new trend:

I have no fear for the race because of the antics of the so-called "flappers."
They may be a little wild, but I venture to say that the average girl today
is just as good as they were in my day. The boys too—although they go
in for some curious fads—will probably make pretty good fathers for the
coming generation.

THE HOMEFRONT

From the city streets to the country lanes, the people of WNY built their homes and raised their families. Not lacking in adventure, residents explored the villages around them and reported back as if on assignment.

August 16, 1910—Buffalo
Here is a great place to raise caine. Artie

May 23, 1910—Akron, NY
Well, Al and I are in Akron—very nice little town with a multitude of pretty girls. We had a fine time last night. Strolled about 10 miles from the feel of my legs today.

April 4, 1909—Albion
This is about the nicest—I mean the lonesomest town I ever was in. The population is about 5,500. There are about 250 ladies at the place we are working but you would get killed if you ever looked at one of them here. There are 2 new boilers that we had to handle and they weigh 12 tons a piece. From your bashful cousin Herman

Sept 23, 1913—Eden
Dear Irene—Eden certainly is a fine place. You must try and come out here some time and stay all night with us. We will have a fine time I know. Love to all. From Kate S. Henel

October 17, 1910—Depew
Hello Charles, did you have a good time yesterday? If convenient for you, would like to have you and Arthur come over Wednesday. We have sent word to Herman. What do you think of Tonawanda? A.H.B.

FOOD FOR THE SOUL

As soon as communities were formed, so was formalized education. Most communities had their own schools, although variations ranged from one-room schoolhouses to separate grammar and high schools. In the country, school was typically held in the spring, summer and fall. The winter months were not deemed suitable as the weather made it impossible for many children to get to school. Recesses would be given at harvest time to allow children to help with the crops.

Higher education had also made its debut in Buffalo by the mid-1800s. The University of Buffalo opened as a private institution in 1846, and Bryant & Stratton College followed in 1854. Buffalo Normal School, now Buffalo State College, opened on Elmwood Avenue in 1871 and became the first public college in Buffalo. The private Medaille College followed in

1875 and D'Youville College in 1908. To meet the needs of the increasingly well-educated population, Buffalo Public Library opened in 1887, and soon libraries began to emerge in smaller communities as well.

Religion in WNY was as varied as its people. In Williamsville, for example, the earliest evidence of formalized religion can be traced to 1807 and a traveling Methodist minister. Soon, the Reformed Mennonite Church opened in 1834 in a stone structure still standing on the corner of Main Street and North Forrest Road. Following this, church buildings were erected by the Catholics, Methodists, Baptists and Lutherans. Williamsville, like most villages in WNY, was a melting pot of faith.

> *May 18, 1910—Snyder*
> *Well cousin, I'll try and come to your house a week from Sunday—I've got to be on deck at S.S. Sunday School. I'm a pretty regular scholar. Ha!*

Opposite: November 18, 1922. Newlyweds John J. Carson Jr. and his bride, Nancy Gardner, lived at 4430 Main Street in Snyder. Their home was a wedding present from Nancy's parents and new neighbors, William Allen and Edith (Sideway) Gardner. *Courtesy of David Carson.*

Above: A September 1901 wedding photo of Mary McNeff Haffey and James Joseph Haffey of Welland, Ontario, Canada. On their honeymoon, they stopped at the Pan-American Exposition. They arrived just days after the death of President William McKinley.

Left: Kathryn Donovan and her big brother, William, pose for a photo during a stroll through their neighborhood on East Utica Street in Buffalo.

Irene and Cyrus Schoelles are dressed in their best for this photo, taken about 1896.

Baby Ruth, daughter of John B. and Dorothy Zink Schoelles, posed for this portrait at C.T. Stumpf in Tonawanda.

The Schoelles family lived in Getzville, near present-day Schoelles Road. Pictured are four of their six children: Katherine, Cyrus, Ruth and Dorothy.

Dressed in his Sunday best, Benjamin George Paulin Jr. poses for his photo to be taken.

Dressed in elegant lace and a wide-rimmed hat, Ella Johnson Paulin is a stunning example of the traditional Victorian portrait.

Dorothy Zink Schoelles elegantly displays a tight, corseted dress with the large bustle so typical of the late 1800s.

James, Antoinette, Hugh, Eileen, Loretto and Mary Haffey of Welland, Ontario. A strong belief in God and family guided their lifestyle. Antoinette soon became a nun and Hugh a priest. Eileen and Loretto married and raised families, Eileen in St. Catherine's and Loretto in WNY.

Photographer Arthur J. Rundle captures the Philip Rundle family on their farm in 1917. The photo illustrates the life of a blended family, as Philip married three times and fathered fourteen children. His youngest was born when he was sixty-six years old. He claimed a baby bonus and old age pension at the same time—an unusual occurrence.

Canadian-born Joseph Rundle raised his family in WNY and became an American citizen himself in 1945.

Sporting the appropriate necktie, this gentleman posed on Humboldt Parkway during the city's golden era.

Above: While attending the 1926 WNY Firemen's Convention in Kenmore, the Snyder Hose Company firefighters sported their dress uniforms. *Courtesy of Snyder Fire Department.*

Right: By the 1920s, the age of the corset and full skirt had been abandoned. As modeled by Ruth and Laura Landel, Russian-style headdresses and long strings of pearls were all the rage.

The age of the flapper saw women bob their hair and expose not only their ankles but also (gasp!) their kneecaps.

Opposite, top: A parade down Main Street in Snyder passes the original Snyder Post Office. Located at the northwest corner of Main Street and Harlem Road, Michael Snyder built this post office for the village that would soon bear his name.

Opposite, middle: William Allen and Edith Gardner, whose ancestors made their money by opening the Buffalo Saving Bank, built a fifty-two-acre estate called Brookfield Farm in 1907. It was located on what is now the Daemen College campus. *Courtesy of David Carson.*

Opposite, bottom: The Carson estate, located on the Gardners' property, was built in 1922 as a wedding gift to their daughter. It was here that the Great Robbery of Amherst took place in 1929. *Courtesy of David Carson.*

The Peffer residence on Buffalo Street in Hamburg.

Arthur Landel's house at 5864 Main Street in Williamsville was purchased from the Hershey family following World War I. Presently, the dwelling is the home of Robitaille Real Estate and retains the original shutters. The carriage house that was once used in Landel's dairy business still remains and is occupied by Maid Brigade.

This house at 554 Humboldt Parkway in Buffalo was torn down while building an onramp to the Kensington Expressway.

This view, taken from the window of 554 Humboldt, shows the parkway before it was divided by the expressway.

Titled "On Our Way to Wilson," the photographer captured a couple out for a Sunday drive.

The view toward Main Street, Clarence, from Ransom Road, just beyond the bridge.

The Erie Canal brought prominence, pride, luxury and crime to the Lockport area. The original structure of the Lockport Courthouse originated in 1886 and was built from Lockport limestone and Ohio sandstone. Replacing a smaller courthouse, it served as a symbol of a growing community and changing times. *Photography by Peter Scumaci.*

This one-room schoolhouse in Wendelville was attended by first grade student Irene Schoelles (front row, fourth from left) in 1897.

Opposite, top: A few years later, Irene (second row, sixth from left) attended this school in Getzville.

Opposite, middle: This turn-of-the-century postcard shows Eden High School.

Opposite, bottom: Built on Academy Street in 1853, the Williamsville Classical Institute was the first in Williamsville to educate beyond the elementary level.

Creating Communities

The Pinewoods School in North Tonawanda, 1884. *Courtesy of NTHM.*

Central High School opened in Buffalo in 1853 and occupied the former Burt Mansion at Franklin and Court Streets. This marked the first time a building was used solely for high school, and it remained Buffalo's only high school until 1897.

Above: Originally serving as Bryant High School in the 1800s, this building in North Tonawanda became Felton Grammar School in 1927, when the new Payne Avenue High School was built. *Courtesy of NTHM.*

Right: Myra Longnecker, shown in her graduation photo, was a proud member of Bryant & Stratton College's class of 1912. Commencement ceremonies were held on June 13 at Convention Hall.

Buffalo Public Library opened in Lafayette Square in 1887. The stunning Romanesque building, designed by architect Cyrus Eidlitz, was razed in 1960 and replaced with the current structure. *Courtesy of TPS.*

Carnegie Library in North Tonawanda was built in 1903. *Courtesy of NTHM.*

Above, left: St. Paul's Lutheran Church in Williamsville was founded in 1869. Pastor Heinrich Rudolf Grabau served from 1896 to 1909 and held all services in German.

Above, right: Charles Landel was confirmed by Pastor Grabau in 1901, just one year after the new church building was dedicated at the corner of Eagle and North Ellicott Streets.

A late 1920s congregational photo shows Pastor Schleifer and his parishioners in front of St. Paul's. While the building has undergone several additions, this main church building still stands.

Left: The Roman Catholic Church of the Ascension was organized in North Tonawanda in 1884 by Father Bustin, who later built the church and parsonage. *Courtesy of NTHM.*

Below: A visiting parishioner sent this postcard from the Methodist Episcopal Church and Parsonage in Akron in 1910.

Chapter 4

TRAVEL AND TRANSPORTATION

During the Gilded Age in WNY, the travel and transportation industry was forever growing and changing. Horse carts and carriages gave way to bicycles and automobiles, stagecoaches made way for trolley cars and railroads connected WNY to the continental United States. Dirt paths evolved into paved roads, and those roads were soon lit by electric lights. Lavish ships traveled back and forth to Canada, and the invention of the airplane made the world a smaller place. Yes, the Gilded Age was full of wonder and invention, and the people of WNY graciously embraced it all.

TROLLEYS AND TRAINS

By the late 1800s, travel by trolley car had become commonplace in WNY. Trolleys carried people to and from the city with unparalleled efficiency and revolutionized the way people traveled. This freedom led to new opportunities for all Western New Yorkers, opening up new markets for consumers and new living possibilities for city workers. In Amherst, for example, the Buffalo and Williamsville Electric Railway was paramount in the growth of the suburbs, as prominent city businessmen looked to these locations to build their "countryside estates." The Gardner family, who rose to prominence through the Buffalo Savings Bank, kept a large estate on Main

Street in Snyder, as did their new neighbor, Arthur Hedstrom, proprietor of Hedstrom Spaulding, one of Buffalo's largest coal distributers.

For the average citizen, trolley travel simply made the world bigger. Beginning in 1918, the International Railway Company (IRC) ran high-speed service to Niagara Falls. In Tonawanda, the IRC also had a "funeral" streetcar, which allowed mourners to accompany the departed directly into Elmlawn Cemetery. Without question, the trolleys opened residents up to more possibilities than ever before, and many wrote of this phenomenon on the penny postcards of the day.

When Herman Landel wrote to his Williamsville cousin Charles, he spoke of his experiences with the trolley—and the ladies:

> *September 29, 1910—Clarence*
> *Dear cousin, you said it wasn't far to Bowmansville Station. I did some very swift walking almost all the way from Transit to the station. I wasn't cooled off yet when I got home. But—I met a dandy little girl on the train and escorted her to a boarding house in Clarence.*

Meanwhile, Charles's fiancée, Irene Schoelles of Getzville, had written the following from her trip to Lockport:

> *July 27, 1910—Lockport*
> *Am having a great time. Try and come Friday about 4 or 5 o'clock and I will meet you at the station.*

For many residents like Irene, visits to nearby communities were made easier by the trolley system. Plans could be made to attend functions that at one time would have been too far of a commute. It was the Gilded Age, and fun and folly were priorities.

> *Dec 22, 1910—Clarence*
> *Dear Cousin—Well I suppose you are waiting breathlessly for x-mas as to give Irene her present. I was in Sunday and had a dandy time. I stayed overnight and took the morning train home. How about the Hutchin Hose Ball? I expect to go. Herm*

For those needing to venture outside of the WNY area, traditional railroad travel was the method of choice. Built in 1848, Buffalo's first true station was housed on Exchange Street and served Cornelius Vanderbilt's railroad empire. Several stations graced the Buffalo landscape in the following years, as WNY became a hub of business and pleasure travel. By the 1880s, leaders had begun to wish for a union station to serve all of the rail traffic in and out of the city. A site in the Fillmore District was selected, but this union station would never come to pass.

By 1925, the city leaders, New York Central Railroad and the Grade Crossing and Terminal Station Commission had finally agreed on the Central Terminal, which was to be built in the Fillmore District, only two and a half miles from the downtown business district. The grand, seventeen-floor building debuted in 1929 and served the community of WNY for the next half century.

Personal Travel

The natural landscape of WNY opened opportunities for many different forms of personal travel. Before the advent of the automobile, early residents employed a wide variety of methods and machinery to get from place to place. In cooperating weather, local waterways were filled with boats of all shapes and sizes, and early roads were graced with carriages and horse carts. Since the conditions of these roads could be affected by pitfalls ranging from impassable mud to extreme dust, the local papers would publish reports and warnings, and private citizens would turn to one another for updates. In a correspondence from Albion to Williamsville, the following was reported:

> *April 4, 1909—Albion*
> *There are some well streets here when they are not muddy. It is all gravel around here. You should see all the muddy buggies—but Otto's is clean. There are so many buggies with two horses. I have enough trouble with one horse when I go out riding, don't you?*

Later that year, a Clarence resident, who planned to travel to Amherst the following week, sent a postcard to a Williamsville friend. It simply contained the following:

> *Nov 9, 1910—Clarence*
> *Is the brick pavement open yet?*

As the snow fell, however, the fashionable choice for both transportation and recreation turned to sleigh rides. While children looked forward to the smooth speed of the cool winter drive and young couples longed to snuggle beneath the blankets on a thick winter's evening, many wrote of the experience in both anticipation and recollection:

Dec 23, 1909—Snyder
A Merry Christmas! We went skating and sliding down Hedstrom's toboggan last night and had an awful snowy sleigh ride tonight. How are your prospects for the 31st? Rather bleak here, R.F.H.

Dec 31, 1909—Buffalo
Thank you for the dandy Christmas card. I am coming out soon so as to get that sleigh ride. Susie

Jan 31, 1910—Buffalo
Well this is Sunday evening 9:45. You ought to have been to the sleigh ride. We had a fine time and had such joy. I got home at 5:30 a.m. & only got an hour's sleep—felt like ooo the next day. H.E.L.

Feb 24, 1909—Snyder
I will write to all of you that barring accidents and setbacks I will come to your house early Friday morning about 9 o'clock. Very nice sleighing isn't it? I suppose you wish there wouldn't be sleighing if I repeat last Sunday's performance don't you? Ha ha. I am sawing wood for exercise nowadays. From your dull cousin

In the warmer months, the bicycle was a mode of transportation and entertainment all its own. Although George N. Pierce had manufactured tricycles on Main Street since 1878, when the first chain-driven bicycle was developed in 1889, Pierce and WNY embraced the new invention wholeheartedly. Soon, Pierce was manufacturing two-wheel bicycles, and droves of Western New Yorkers wheeled about on these new contraptions. By the turn of the century, many were enjoying the Parkside Wheeling Club, and the bicycle had become a viable mode of transportation on the WNY roadways.

THE AUTOMOBILE AND AIRPLANE

Following the turn of the century, the age of the automobile began. Soon, "gas buggies" were not just a novelty for the wealthy, and the landscape of WNY roadways changed forever. In the earliest days, many considered those with autos foolish, and jeers of "Get a horse!" could be heard every time one suffered a breakdown on community streets. For others, autos were considered appropriate for recreation but not suitable for "dependable work."

> *August 3, 1910—Depew*
> *How's the boy today? Saturday I took a ride on the motor—went about 40 miles. Suppose you did a little driving yesterday too. Was a fine day. Alvin*

Over time, however, the automobiles on the street would slowly eclipse the number of horse carriages, and residents would officially trade the smell of fertilizer for the equally potent smell of exhaust.

In addition to the motorcar revolution, the turn of the century also marked the birth of the airplane. After playing an important role in World War I, the aircraft became a curiosity for the American public. Luckily, experienced fighter pilots, known as barnstormers, were eager to show off their skills. Visiting towns across the country, the pilots would give demonstrations and take paying passengers for a ride.

The Buffalo & Williamsville Electric Railway was affectionately known as the "Toonerville Trolley." It is pictured on Main Street near Glen Falls in Williamsville.

An original ticket and a token from the "Toonerville Trolley" show a departure time of 8:00 a.m. During its heyday, the trolley ran every twelve minutes and carried over four hundred passengers each day. *Courtesy of Kevin Maria.*

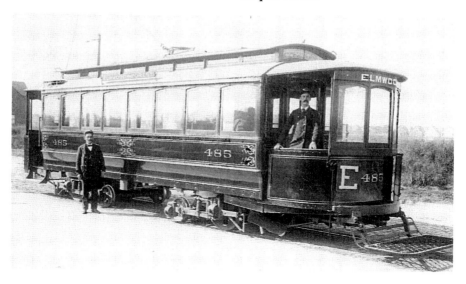

Pictured with the Elmwood streetcar #485 are two of its proud conductors. A fine specimen, this closed-car trolley was an improvement over similar open-car models. *Courtesy of TPS.*

Children play about this idle trolley car, which appears to have traveled along the lakeshore.

New York Central Station, Buffalo. During the later part of the nineteenth century, Buffalo was a primary gateway for commerce to and from the west. The New York Central and Hudson River Railroads were very profitable.

The large number of Buffalo railroads provided honest work for numerous WNY citizens of the nineteenth and early twentieth centuries. The Lehigh Valley Terminal was built on lower Main Street in 1910. *Courtesy of TPS.*

Opposite, top: Tonawanda's railroad station was built on Main Street at Fletcher and Grove Streets in 1870 and served as a regular stop on New York Central's Niagara Falls line.

Opposite, bottom: This snapshot from the early twentieth century was captioned: "Sailing on the Niagara."

Beulah (Snyder) Fiddler enjoys a float down Ellicott Creek in Getzville in the mid-1920s.

Opposite, top: The silhouette of Charles Landel and his one-horse buggy is seen on a winter's day. Landel's grandparents settled in Tonawanda after emigrating from France. They operated a farm on the Erie Canal.

Marshall Thompson rides through the WNY streets in a chauffer-driven carriage.

Above: Snow falls as this sleighing party gets ready for adventure.

Left: Leroy Arenz displays a two-wheel, chain-driven bicycle, a hearty improvement over the "ordinary bicycle," which employed a huge front wheel with attached pedals.

Bicycles became commonplace in the city of Buffalo and opened up new modes of business, including Western Union's telegraph boys.

This postcard of the auto parade at Luna Park was postmarked 1910.

The Paulin family out for a leisurely Sunday drive.

The Dunkles enjoyed taking a drive in their new Ford.

Travel and Transportation

Right: Earl and Beulah Fiddler captured this image of a family friend posing with her new auto in front of the Albright Knox Art Gallery.

Below: Enthusiasts would never refuse a chance to build a recreational auto out of spare parts.

Above: This touring car, labeled "the Stripper," was complete with a storage box on the running boards.

Left: "Fiddler's New Buick." This car was believed to be an improvement over his previous Ford model.

The Maxwell Company, founded in 1904 in Tarrytown, New York, was sold to Chrysler in 1925. In addition to Clara Landel, Jack Benny also drove a Maxwell.

This early "limousine" was used for pictures after carrying a large party to a picnic in the country. It was said to seat eight to ten.

Snyder Hose Company's Ahrens-Fox Fire Pumper is shown on its Main Street parade route in 1925.

Ben Paulin and his mother, Ella, pose by their automobile and a Mobil Gas billboard.

Opposite: Beulah Snyder and Ruth Schoelles enjoy an aircraft visiting Delaware Park in the 1920s.

Beulah Snyder and Ruth Schoelles enjoy an aircraft visiting Delaware Park in the 1920s.

Chapter 5
LUXURY AND LEISURE

The Gilded Age in WNY marked a time of leisure, play and hobbies. People enjoyed the theatre, traveling, boating, camping, hotel stays and visiting places like Crystal Beach in Canada. WNY was a tourist adventure land, and the art of photography elegantly captured the historical and social events of the time.

PHOTOGRAPHY

Early WNY photographers made a comfortable living and became important inventors of the trade. Charles Pond, remembered for his photographic stereoviews, produced his first in 1867. The stereoview captured the Buffalo Lighthouse and people stranded in the Buffalo Harbor due to a May ice jam. George Eastman founded Eastman Kodak in Rochester in 1880. In 1901, he introduced a camera for amateur use—a box roll-film camera. The camera cost one dollar and was easy enough for children to use. Eastman is credited with the explosion of widespread photography due to this invention.

Jacob Riis was famous for photojournalism about 1890. He worked in New York City taking photos of the poor, immigrants and slums and published a book titled *How the Other Half Lives*. Riis is known for using flash powder photography and taking indoor photographs. While serving as the police commissioner of New York City, Theodore Roosevelt occasionally accompanied Riis on photo shoots.

OLMSTED PARKS

America's first landscape architect, Frederick Law Olmsted, is well known for the impact he made in WNY. Olmsted came to the area in the late 1800s and created a park system for the City of Buffalo. The design creatively connected the six parks he designed—Cazenovia Park, Delaware Park, Front Park, Riverside Park, South Park and Humboldt Park (now Martin Luther King Jr. Park)—through a series of parkways. Still used today, Olmsted's parks remain a spectacular reminder of WNY's gilded past.

> *July 5, 1910—Clarence*
> *Well Charles, I didn't get to the picnic did I? I will explain. I had as nice time as could be desired the other night—all but the dancing. I danced as trifle on the lawn but it wasn't very nice. I am way behind in the sleep line. Sunday night we got home at 3am and last night at 1am. I was in the 7th heaven of delight yesterday. I will be out to see you sooner or later and explain.*

OVERNIGHT STAYS

During the Gilded Age, travel and adventure were commonplace. With personal travel taking place by horse and buggy or newfangled automobiles, tourists made frequent stops along their journeys. Buffalo's position along the canal and waterways also made WNY a prime spot for layovers. In choosing lodging, being pampered was important for many travelers. To accommodate this, the Hotel Markeen had 180 home-like rooms and advertized being a fireproof lodging with reasonable rates and a garage. It was also credited with having the finest dining room in WNY.

The Hotel Lenox was built in 1896 as an eight-story apartment building. It is thought that it was converted to a hotel about 1900 in preparation for the tourist business expected for the Pan-American Exposition. The hotel provided an electric carriage service for its guests. It was known as being fashionable and catered to travelers, tourists and "permanent guests." Today, people still enjoy being pampered in luxurious hotels in the Buffalo area. The Mansion on Delaware Avenue is a prime example.

For others, the lure of the campfire was stronger than that of fancy hotels. With much of WNY still undeveloped, campers had plenty of prime locations from which to choose. With the advent of the automobile, people were able to travel more efficiently and explore natural wonders once out of reach for a quick getaway.

FUN AT THE BEACH

Travel to Canada took place by boat and by bridge. With places like Crystal Beach, Canada was an alluring location for a holiday. Tourists could relax on the beach, mingle in the dance hall or enjoy the rides. The sea walk provided entertainment, food, photos, games and priceless memories to write home about.

July 28, 1913—Crystal Beach Ontario
Don't you wish you were here? This week is nice and warm and I am sunburned on my back. Will see you soon. Edith

July 11, 1910—Crystal Beach Ontario
You ought to be with Ray and I now! Have not found anyone yet, but are hopeful—lots of girls here. Boats are running my ideas. Don't believe we will see home tonight. Alvin

In 1925, the building of the five-arch Peace Bridge that connects Buffalo to Canada began. The budget for the project was $4.5 million and was completed in the spring of 1927. The first drive across the bridge took place on March 13 by the project engineer, Edward Lupfer. The Peace Bridge opened to the public on June 1 and was dedicated on August 7. The international ceremony was attended by U.S. vice president Charles Dawes, as well as Edward, Prince of Wales, and his brother, the future King George.

OUT AND ABOUT IN WNY

The Buffalo Yacht Club, located on Porter Avenue in Buffalo, opened in 1860 with only twelve members. An initiation fee of three dollars and dues of two dollars were small prices to pay for such status. Many prominent people have belonged to the club, including President Grover Cleveland. Fire and storms destroyed the first four yacht club buildings.

An interest in acting and entertainment was a sign of the times. Local theatres and acting groups grew in popularity, and vaudeville ruled the day. Born in Ontario, Canada, Michael Shea opened a series of successful theatres in Buffalo and Toronto, employing such acts as W.C. Fields, the Four Cohans (with George M. Cohan, of course) and Joe, Myra and Buster Keaton.

Beyond the theatre, community members spent their leisure time enjoying a variety of events and activities. Automobiles, parks, baseball, zoos and YMCAs became important parts of our culture, social life and history. In captured moments like these, the WNY of one hundred years ago can look remarkably similar to the WNY of today. Yes, the contributions of the Gilded Age are poignantly evident and forever preserved in some of WNY's greatest treasures.

Opposite, top: An advertisement for the artistic photography of R.W. Lande of Lockport.

Opposite, bottom: Children's Day in Delaware Park was a popular community event. *Courtesy of TPS.*

Strolling through the beautiful Rose Garden in Delaware Park.

Skating on the lake in Delaware Park was an enjoyable winter adventure. Surviving the winter in WNY meant enjoying outdoor recreation.

In addition to skating, sledding provided great entertainment. Note the wooden toboggan shoot in the background.

Visitors exit the Delaware Park Casino after a long day in the park.

Following their visit, friends pose for a picture on the casino's porch.

The Hotel Markeen was a popular place to enjoy a meal. Decorated with glorious chandeliers, high ceilings and intricate designs, the hotel was an elegant place to visit. *Courtesy of TPS.*

The Blue Parlor in the Buffalo Hotel Lenox shows the Victorian flare of the time period.

The Mansion on Delaware is a glorious location for a vacation, a wedding reception or a meeting place. *Photography by Peter Scumaci.*

A postcard of the grand Genesee Hotel in 1906. *Courtesy of TPS.*

Travelers pose for a souvenir photo outside of a bed-and-breakfast that welcomes visitors.

Evelyn McRae, Kathryn Paulin and Mac McRae pose on the boardwalk for a photo near their hotel on a leisurely getaway.

Beulah Snyder and friends explore Ellicott Creek in Getzville.

Opposite, top: Sisters Beulah, Gladys and Agnes Snyder enjoy a summer camping trip with their fellas.

Opposite, middle: Circling the fire for some warmth and a spot of coffee.

Opposite, bottom: Clara Landel explores the creek near Genesee Street.

Left: Friends wade in the waters of Ellicott Creek after a leisurely canoe ride.

Below: Nancy Gardner Carson, dressed in her pearls, poses for a photo on a beautiful summer day in 1928. *Courtesy of David Carson.*

Opposite, top: A group, including Gladys Snyder and Earl and Beulah Fiddler, celebrates the new Peace Bridge.

Opposite, middle: Every day, boatloads of tourists sailed across Lake Ontario and docked in Canada for a holiday at Crystal Beach. The vessel also transported the mail from one country to the other. *Courtesy of TPS.*

Opposite, bottom: Train rides at Crystal Beach left from Buffalo's Union Station, illustrating the importance of the Buffalo and Canadian connection.

Above: The scenic beauty and attractions at Crystal Beach. Imagine riding a wooden roller coaster so close to the water.

Left: Laura and Eva Landel are all dressed up and ready to be escorted to the dance hall.

Ella Johnson poses with a friend for a photo while vacationing at Crystal Beach. Their dresses and shoes highlight the fashion of the time.

A backdrop on the boardwalk at Crystal Beach is an ideal spot to stop for a souvenir photo. Friends pose with apples, flowers and smiles. *Courtesy of TPS.*

Opposite, top: Mothers, daughters and friends pose in their bathing suits on the beach in 1913. The long bathing suits and bathing caps illustrate the modesty of the time.

Opposite, bottom: Family vacation fun at Crystal Beach. Benjamin Paulin Jr. stops swimming to pose for a photo with his mother, Ella, and a friend.

Above: Fun prevailed as this quartet pose for a pyramid photo on the beach.

Right: Earl Fiddler (right) and friends enjoy summer fun and frolicking.

Eva and Bill are head over heels in love in the fun and sun.

Opposite: Eva and Bill are head over heels in love in the fun and sun.

Above: A postcard of the Buffalo Yacht Club on Lake Ontario. *Courtesy of TPS.*

Right: Ahoy mates!

A photo of the Buffalo Yacht Club as it stands in 2010. The American and Canadian flags fly high in the distance. The Peace Bridge can be seen in the background. *Photography by Peter Scumaci.*

Above, top: The Riviera Theatre opened on December 30, 1926, and was billed as the "Showplace of the Tonawandas." *Courtesy of NTHM.*

Above, bottom: On opening night, admission to the Riviera Theatre cost one dollar, and patrons enjoyed movies and vaudeville acts. The theatre is still enjoyed by audiences today. *Courtesy of NTHM.*

Opposite, bottom: Shea's Theatre on Main Street in Buffalo opened in 1925 as a result of the motion picture boom. The theatre's marquis dazzled with seven thousand electric lights on the night of its premier. *Photography by Peter Scumaci.*

The Audubon Players, a local theatre group, pose for a cast photo.

Reverend Henry Schleifer poses outside of the prestigious Albright Knox Art Gallery, which opened in 1905.

Opposite, top: A beautiful water fountain and bandstand decorate Russell Park in Akron.

Opposite, middle: A Buffalo Bisons baseball team photo taken in 1878. By 1880, the Bisons had played eighty-two games at Riverside Grounds with a record of twenty-four wins and fifty-eight losses. *Courtesy of TPS.*

Opposite, bottom: Entertaining crowds since 1875, the Buffalo Zoological Gardens is the third oldest zoo in the United States. *Courtesy of TPS.*

The YMCA building in North Tonawanda was built in 1892 and also housed the city hall, jail and police department. *Courtesy of NTHM.*

Lusk's Pond in Clarence was a beautiful place to relax and enjoy nature.

Chapter 6

WATERFALLS AND WONDERS

The early communities of WNY had the luxury of enjoying many outstanding waterfalls and natural wonders. No matter what their coordinates, early WNY residents were only minutes away from spectacular scenes that could be appreciated for both their beauty and functionality.

NIAGARA FALLS

According to local folklore, the word *Niagara* was derived from the Iroquois Indian word *Onguiaahra*, meaning "the strait." Stemming from the Niagara River, the Niagara Falls area is categorized by three waterfalls: the American Falls, the Bridal Veil Falls and the Horseshoe Falls. While the American and Bridal Veil Falls are part of the New York State Park system, the Horseshoe Falls belongs to our Canadian neighbors and is also known as the Canadian Falls.

A few distinct events can be credited with the popular growth of the Niagara Falls area. First, the development of the rail system in the early 1800s made Niagara Falls accessible to visitors and enticed travelers from all over the world. In fact, Napoleon Bonaparte's younger brother, Jerome, took his American bride to Niagara Falls on their honeymoon in 1804 and is often credited with starting this tradition, which earned Niagara Falls the moniker "honeymoon capital of the world."

When the Erie Canal connected the Hudson River with Lake Erie in 1825, it opened up another means to reach the Niagara area. In later years, that same area would serve as a northern terminus of the Underground Railroad. While professional slave catchers patrolled the Niagara River searching for escaped slaves, locals would hide them in secret cellars and tunnels until it was safe to pass to Canada.

During the Industrial Revolution, eager businessmen began to construct mills and factories along the Niagara River. By the late 1860s, concerned citizens had begun to worry about salvaging the natural beauty of the Greater Niagara area. The small group formed the Free Niagara Movement, which campaigned for the preservation of the area. Under the guidance of America's first landscape architect, Frederick Law Olmsted, the Niagara Reservation was born in 1885.

Despite its designation as a state park, the power of the Niagara River could still be used to produce electricity. In the same year that the Niagara received its park designation, the Edward Dean Adams Hydroelectric Generating Station opened. This station was the world's first commercial-scale producer of alternating current, the first current that could be sent great distances.

The allure and power of Niagara Falls enticed several early daredevils to execute death-defying stunts. The first person to be credited with going over the falls in a barrel, however, was a sixty-three-year-old female schoolteacher from Michigan. On October 24, 1901, Annie Edson Taylor emerged from her ride over the falls bleeding but virtually unharmed. Upon exiting the barrel, Taylor told the world's media: "No one should ever try that again." Apparently, those words were lost on Bobby Leach, who became the second person, and the first male, to go over the falls. Following his stunt on July 25, 1911, Leach spent six months in the hospital recovering from his injuries, which were reported to include two broken kneecaps and a fractured jaw.

The harsh winters of WNY can also create some interesting situations at Niagara Falls. For instance, the only time that the flow of water stopped completely over each of the falls was on March 29, 1848. While the falls themselves did not actually freeze over, an ice jam in the upper river stopped the flow of water. Whether brave or crazy, many people actually walked out onto the dry rocks and recovered artifacts from the riverbed.

If the winter was cold enough, ice could accumulate across the river and form an ice bridge. This bridge could extend for miles downriver, not breaking apart until it reached the lower rapids of the falls. Prior to 1912, visitors were able to walk out onto the ice bridge and stand beneath the falls. On February 24, 1888, the local paper reported that at least twenty thousand people had walked or tobogganed on the ice that winter. The site was so popular that shanties were constructed along the riverbank, enabling tourists to buy liquor, have photos taken or purchase souvenirs. Tragically, the annual party on the ice bridge was forever terminated on February 4, 1912, when three tourists perished after the ice bridge broke and the crowds fell into the icy water below.

Glen Falls

Located off Main Street in the village of Williamsville, Glen Park is home to another of WNY's great waterfalls. Born from the waters of Ellicott Creek tumbling over the Onondaga Escarpment, Glen Falls has been home to many early mills and the subject of countless images throughout the centuries. Appreciated for both its functionality and its beauty, Glen Falls and the surrounding park became a popular destination for community members and tourists alike.

Since Williamsville was a convenient sleepover spot for early travelers to the northern regions of WNY, many nature lovers would stop by Glen Falls before their ultimate destination of Niagara Falls. A postcard sent to Clinton Street in New York City recounts the following from one couple's sightseeing trip:

> *May 28, 1916—Buffalo*
> *We got as close as 15 miles. This is the Eagle House Hotel at Williamsville where we are now. We are going to Niagara Falls tomorrow if nothing happens. It doesn't seem very far.*

A postcard sent to Detroit, this one sporting a picture of a cascading Glen Falls on the front, said the following of the author's adventure:

> *Aug 11, 1915—Williamsville*
>
> *Grand trip,*
> *Grand place,*

Grand auto-rides,
Grand weather, (I'm knocking wood)
Grand Time,
Grand EATS (+ getting fat???).
Laura

THE LETCHWORTH FALLS

William Pryor Letchworth became a partner in Pratt and Letchworth at age twenty-five. A malleable iron business, the firm was located in Buffalo and was, according to the 1872 *New York Times*, "the largest manufacturer of saddlery hardware in the United States." Once his Buffalo affairs were in order, Letchworth set forth on a mission of self-discovery. Looking to escape the commotion of city life, Letchworth stepped off a local railcar one day and found himself on the Portage Bridge of the Genesee. As the other tourists marveled at the falls below, Letchworth knew he had found his new home. In 1859, Letchworth purchased the land surrounding the Portage Falls and began construction of his Glen Iris Estate. Soon, famous landscape artist William Webster was designing winding paths and strategically placing lakes and fountains. Stone stairs and walkways were built beside the upper, middle and lower falls, and a spotlight was eventually positioned to shine nightly on the twenty-seven-foot drop of the middle falls.

Letchworth himself worked tirelessly to preserve the natural history of this land, which the Seneca Indians had called *Sehgehunda*. He moved an ancient council house to a bluff above his estate and created the Council Grounds. The grounds were baptized at the Council Fire on October 1, 1872. The evening involved speeches by the Senecas and the Iroquois and the rededication of the council house. The festivities concluded with the Native Americans and other guests, among whom was former president Millard Fillmore, planting memorial trees.

Letchworth never married, but his Glen Iris Estate was always full of visitors and friends. He continued his preservation efforts by building a museum to house the natural artifacts collected in the region. In 1906, Letchworth donated his thousand-acre estate to the State of New York, and Letchworth State Park was born in 1907. Letchworth continued to live at the

Glen Iris Estate until his death in 1910. Although many people expected that he would wish to spend eternity on the grounds he so deeply loved, William Pryor Letchworth chose to be buried at Forest Lawn Cemetery beneath a plain slab of stone from his Lower Falls.

Above: This image, taken from the American side of the park, shows Niagara Falls and the early twentieth-century viewing area at the precipice.

Right: Unaware of the unpredictable current that the Niagara could produce, this mother lets her infant play in the water downriver from the falls in the early 1900s.

Taken in the 1920s, this photo shows gentlemen enjoying a day of sightseeing at Niagara Falls State Park.

As it was considered a very fashionable place for families and friends to gather, it is reported that the Vanderbilts proposed using the present Goat Island section of the park as a pleasure ground for passengers riding their trains to Niagara Falls.

Former Barnum and Bailey Circus performer Bobby Leach went over Niagara Falls in a barrel in 1911. Prior to his stunt, Leach owned a restaurant on Bridge Street and would boast to customers about how he would one day navigate the falls. *Courtesy of TPS.*

This photo, taken on February 19, 1909, shows some adventurous tourists standing on the frozen waters atop Niagara Falls, dangerously close to the precipice.

A wintry Niagara Falls was nicknamed the Ice Mountain at the time of this photo. On this day, the ice bridge supported a great number of tourists and thrill-seekers alike.

On January 27, 1938, the Honeymoon Bridge collapsed into the Niagara Gorge. Closed in anticipation of the collapse, the bridge buckled due to pressure from the accumulation of ice in the gorge below the falls.

This turn-of-the-century photograph shows Glen Falls and one of the surrounding mills. The top half of the current Creekview Restaurant building can be seen near the top right corner. *Courtesy of Kevin Maria.*

Even in the winter months, Glen Falls was a popular destination for WNY residents and visitors. Here, a friend of Beulah Snyder poses next to the frozen falls.

Opposite, top: This image shows a virtually dry Glen Falls, circa 1908. Pictured are Irene, Dorothy (baby), Dorothy (mother), Ruth and Eleanor Schoelles, Amelia and Will Thuersan and Amelia Oswald.

Opposite, bottom: Irene Schoelles and Amelia Oswald are seated next to a smaller waterfall that ran to the right of the main falls, directly next to the Williamsville Mill.

Above: Before the land surrounding the falls was manually altered with trails, walkways and bridges, early sightseers would have to maneuver some pretty dangerous terrain in order to reach their destination.

Left: The Middle Falls of Letchworth State Park, perhaps the most beautiful of the three, is accessed by descending a set of stone stairs. *Photography by Peter Scumaci.*

144

Waterfalls and Wonders

Above, top: The Portage Bridge and falls are seen in this early 1900s postcard. It is this view that first enticed future owner William Pryor Letchworth to move to the area.

Above, middle: Following its 1907 designation, the park became a tremendous tourist attraction, as everyone wanted a glimpse of the infamous William Letchworth estate.

Above, bottom: Park visitors could enter this historic cabin and enjoy the collection of natural artifacts that Letchworth had acquired. This site is still open today.

The Glen Iris Estate was a fine piece of architecture and was enjoyed by Letchworth's many friends. Pictured is the library at this estate.

The Glen Iris Estate, built from the remains of a previous two-story house, had a spectacular view of the Middle Falls from its side porch. Since 1914, the house has served as the Glen Iris Inn, which features fine dining and luxury guest rooms. *Photography by Peter Scumaci.*

THE CIRCLE OF LIFE

No matter where one looks around WNY, a discerning eye can spot the lasting legacy of its Gilded Age. Modern citizens walk the same streets, work in the same buildings and root for the same teams. We enjoy the legacy of the Theatre District, Olmsted's parks and Niagara's wonder. We cherish the memories of those who gave their lives to make our world a better place and strive to carry on the traditions they have left behind. The ghosts of our past are everywhere—and if we are lucky, our ghosts will walk with them down the streets we have all been privileged to call home.

FOREST LAWN CEMETERY

Nowhere are WNY's ghosts more alive than in Forest Lawn Cemetery. Designed as a parklike refuge, modern-day visitors can tour the grounds on foot or through guided trolley tours. Its residents' names read like a prominent guest list from WNY's history, and visitors benefit from the splendor and excess of their gilded past.

THE ERIE CANAL

Any honest account of WNY's history must both begin and end with the Erie Canal. More than any single landmark, event or natural wonder, the Erie Canal symbolizes WNY's Gilded Age. It helped our city rise to prominence and our suburbs grow and prosper. Although its workload has decreased, its legacy lingers—and its impact is eternal.

The "Little Girl" on Mirror Lake stands in memory of all children and showcases the common spirit that ties the WNY community together. *Photography by Peter Scumaci.*

Young Tacie Fargo's monument is a lasting tribute to children of the Gilded Age. *Photography by Peter Scumaci.*

Left: Roswell Park's legacy lives on in Roswell Park Cancer Institute, one of the leading cancer research centers in the country. *Photography by Peter Scumaci.*

Below: Frank Lloyd Wright designed the Blue Sky Mausoleum in honor of his friend Darwin D. Martin. *Photography by Peter Scumaci.*

Tourists pose for a photo after watching a boat navigate the locks.

Nathan Roberts designed the twin flight of locks in 1823. The locks were crucial to the success of the Erie Canal due to the sixty-foot drop. This angle shows the Lockport locks and towpath heading from Albany toward Buffalo. *Photography by Peter Scumaci.*

Bibliography

Books and Articles

Cutter, William Richard. *Genealogical and Family History of Western New York.* New York: Lewis Historical Publishing Company, 1912. Available online through Google Books.

Miller Young, Sue. *History of the Town of Amherst.* Amherst, NY: Town Board of Amherst, 1965.

Reisem, Richard O., and Andy Olenick. *Classic Buffalo: A Heritage of Distinguished Architecture.* Buffalo, NY: Canisius College Press, 2000.

Rossi, Dale T., and Paul F. Redding. "C.L. Pond of Buffalo, NY: Pioneer Stereo Photographer." *Western New York Heritage* 2, no. 1 (Spring 1998): 41–54.

Websites

Baseball Almanac, http://www.baseball-almanac.com/teamstats/roster.php?y=1890&t=BFP

Bridges over Niagara Falls, http://www.niagarafrontier.com/bridges.html#b17

Buffalo Architecture and History, http://buffaloah.com

Buffalo History Works, http://www.buffalohistoryworks.com

Buffalo Olmsted Parks Conservancy, http://www.bfloparks.org

Buffalo Police Then and Now, http://www.bpdthenandnow.com/panamerican.html

Buffalo Yacht Club, http:/www.buffaloyachtclub.org/viewCustomPage.aspx?id=9

"Doing the Pan," http://panam1901.org/index.html

Fulbright American Studies Institute, http://www.uic.edu/depts/oee/fasi/riissequence.html

Harvard University Library Open Collections Program, http://ocp.hul.harvard.edu

Historic Lockport, http://www.elockport.com

Historic Markers, Monuments and Memorials in Buffalo, http://www.andrle.com/markers/mark.htm

Kodak Collector's Page, http://www.nwmangum.com/Kodak/index.html

Letchworth State Park, http://www.letchworthpark.com

Lincoln Legacy, http://mcclurgmuseum.org/legacy/panels/bedell.html

Niagara USA, http://www.niagara-usa.com

NYFalls.com, http://nyfalls.com/glenfalls.html

Photo.net, http://photo.net/history/timeline

Sleaford Museum Trust, http://sleafordmuseum.org.uk/site/musings/article8.html

State of New York Annual Report, 1931, http://www.dmna.state.ny.us/historic/research/AG_Reports/AG_Report_1931.pdf

NEWSPAPERS

Buffalo News

Buffalo Sunday Times

Courier Express

New York Times

INTERVIEWS/DIARIES

Beulah Fiddler

Loretto Rundle

ABOUT THE AUTHORS

Julianna Fiddler-Woite is the great-great-granddaughter of Michael Snyder, namesake of Snyder, New York. In 2009, she published *Snyder, New York: A Brief History*, a more complete supplement to *Snyderville: History of a Village, Portrait of a Family* (1997, out of print). Julianna is a local college instructor who specializes in educational research and writing. As an educator, she enjoys giving presentations on local history to schoolchildren and community groups. Julianna is also a full-time mom, living in Snyder with her husband and four children.

Mary Beth Paulin Scumaci is a lifelong resident of Western New York. Born and raised in Lockport, she is a canawler by birthright. Mary Beth is a New York State certified elementary school teacher and a clinical assistant professor with the School of Education at Medaille College in Buffalo, New York. She enjoys teaching children and graduate students who are studying to become teachers. She specializes in research, writing and online instruction. Mary Beth views this project as a way to make local history come alive for children and teachers. She lives with her family in Williamsville, New York.

Peter C. Scumaci is a New York State certified high school social studies teacher and part-time photographer. His photographs have appeared in local newspapers, on websites, in yearbooks and in family living rooms, as well as in Fiddler-Woite's previous History Press publication. Peter's passion for photography, combined with his extensive knowledge of history, influences his photography. As an educator for over fifteen years, he values the importance of learning and teaching about history in the local community. Peter lives with his family in Williamsville, New York.

The authors, Julianna Fiddler-Woite, Mary Beth Paulin Scumaci and Peter C. Scumaci, enjoy a relaxing moment by the waterfall in Glen Park in honor of the history of Western New York's Gilded Age.